ANOTHER 75 WAYS TO LIVEN UP YOUR TRAINING

A second collection of energizing activities

Another 75 Ways to Liven Up Your Training

A second collection of energizing activities

MARTIN ORRIDGE

Illustrated by Simon Jarvis

Gower

Published by
Gower Publishing Limited
Gower House
Croft Road
Aldershot
Hampshire GU11 3HR
England

Gower
Old Post Road
Brookfield
Vermont 05036
USA

Martin Orridge has asserted his right under the Copyright, Designs and Patents Act 1988 to be identified as the author of this work.

British Library Cataloguing in Publication Data
Orridge, Martin, 1947–
   Another 75 ways to liven up your training : a second collection of energising activities
   1. Employees – Training of   2. Teams in the workplace – Training of
   I. Title   II. Another seventy-five ways to liven up your training
   658.3'12'404

ISBN 0 566 08152 0

Library of Congress Cataloging-in-Publication Data
Orridge, Martin, 1947–
    Another 75 ways to liven up your training : a second collection of energizing activities / Martin Orridge ; illustrated by Simon Jarvis.
      p.   cm.
    ISBN 0–566–08152–0
    1. Employees–Training of–Problems, exercises, etc.   2. Training.
   I. Title.   II. Title: Another seventy-five ways to liven up your training.
   HF5549.5.T70774   1999
   658.3'124–dc21   98–45607
                                                                 CIP

Typeset in Palatino by IML Typographers, Chester and printed in Great Britain at the University Press, Cambridge.

Contents

Preface

Having a success poses the problem whether or not one can produce a successful sequel. We can all remember the many successful films that spawned a family of hideous offspring so I felt a little trepidation when Gower asked me to write a follow up to *75 Ways to Liven Up Your Training*. Did I have enough material? Would friends and colleagues rally round yet again to fill the gaps in my knowledge? ('Is it raw or hard boiled eggs that are thrown?') Do I retain the same format and how can I make it better than the original?

After some thought I concluded that this problem was no different from that faced by any person or organization wishing to improve its performance. After all, I give advice on how to improve organizational performance, so why not take some of my own medicine and use friends and colleagues in the role of my consultants'? The approach worked and once the writing started it soon took shape and you can now judge the end result for yourself.

Since the publication of *75 Ways* a number of people have asked me if and how I use my book. I suppose I have an advantage because a number of the exercises are permanently etched into my brain. However, I often refer to the book at the design stage of a training event and when my colleagues ask me to have something 'up my sleeve' during workshop or similar sessions. Like all people developers I am always prepared to conduct an exercise at no notice. To this end I usually carry Post-its®, string, matches, and sometimes even a jar of coffee beans in my briefcase just in case I have to create something. Having a bag full of odds and ends for your training event can cause 'interesting' problems when passing through airport security, as I once discovered at Heathrow. Fortunately being a management developer seemed to be the correct explanation for having a vacuum flask top, shuttlecock, cocktail stirrers, pieces of string, and a WC handle, etc. in my hand luggage. I have always wondered what it must have looked like on the X-ray machine.

As with *75 Ways* writing this sequel would not have been possible without the continued encouragement and support of my family, friends, drinking partners, and colleagues. For this I thank them and for their tolerance in listening to me as I talked at length about the exercises.

Martin Orridge

Introduction

To help you select the appropriate event, the exercises in this book are grouped according to type or function. Within each exercise, the material is presented in a standard sequence: a description of the exercise, an explanation of its purpose, a list of the materials required, the approximate duration of the exercise, details of the procedure, review suggestions, and some variations on the theme. This information will be of use during the planning and execution phases.

An explanation of each element is given below.

Description   This is a brief overview of what happens during the exercise.

Purpose   This section explains the reason for the exercise. For example, the purpose may be to develop a skill or just to get people working with each other.

Materials   A list of what you need to run the exercise is given here. The requirements are sometimes very specific. At other times, it is up to the trainer to choose a set of materials, and the choice will depend on what is available. I often just look around and see what resources are close to hand. Simply changing some of the materials can give a new edge to an exercise you have used a number of times.

Duration   Approximate timings are given for each exercise. These average figures can easily fluctuate by 50 per cent either way. Human beings are not machines, and they can be very unpredictable. I once lost almost an hour during an important role play when my co-trainer, who was supposed to start the exercise, fell asleep in his room. The participants thought that his non-appearance was an initiative exercise, and had a great deal of fun attempting to work out how the exercise should start. My watchword is 'do not be ruled by the clock'. Always be prepared for the unexpected, and try to use it to your advantage.

Procedure   This section is a step by step guide to running the exercise. Do not just read out the steps to the participants. Make notes, and then add your own flavour to the exercise. Better still, extend the exercise, and make it your own.

Review   A review of the exercise is optional. Sometimes a group discussion is just not appropriate, particularly if the participants have been under a great deal of stress and the team members need to discuss what has happened among themselves. This section gives some pointers as to the types of discussion you could lead. However, the participants are human beings, and they may have learnt something that is quite different from what you expected. Be flexible, and there should be no problems.

Variations   Options for modifications to the exercise are listed here.

I

Ice Breakers

The dog-eared *Concise Oxford Dictionary of current English* (Fifth edition) that my parents gave to me when I embarked on my degree course in the 1960s still provides an excellent definition of the Ice breaker. Ice, *break the* – (fig.) make a beginning, break through reserve or stiffness. This is precisely what the exercises endeavour to achieve throughout this section.

When people are brought together for the first time there is always, as a colleague of mine likes to describe it, a 'sniffing' phase. It is a time of low energy when we suss out each other. We are reserved and stiff, yet if any serious work is going to be completed by the group these barriers have to be removed as quickly as possible. The formal 'round the table' introductions often only serve to reinforce this reserved behaviour. Breaking the ice, rather than a slowly melting the ice approach, can help provide the energy the start of an event requires.

This section provides a number of exercises to help break that ice and provide an impetus to the beginning of an event. Many of them can also be used at any time during the event solely to help raise energy levels among the participants. There is nothing worse than having to work with a group which is drained. To me it feels like punching a huge dense sponge: it takes a great deal of effort but makes no impression. A change of pace can work wonders to liven up even the densest of sponges.

1   Chain Links

Description   Participants meet each other whilst they complete a chain of instructions.

Purpose   A short energizing ice breaking exercise.

Materials   Prepared set of instructions.
A prepared instruction sheet and pencil per participant.

Duration   10 minutes.

Procedure   1.   Prepare a chain of instructions in advance of the event. An example chain might be

You are a motor car.   Find a potato.
You are a potato.   Find a telephone.
You are a telephone.   Find a tea bag.
You are a tea bag.   Find a wheelbarrow.
You are a wheelbarrow.   Find a burnt sausage.
You are a burnt sausage.   Find a motor car.

The list is as long as the number of participants and could be humorous or incorporate items associated with the event or organization. Amusing or unusual items often work best.
2.   Having prepared the list write each line as a separate instruction at the top of each sheet of paper. For example, You are a motor car. Find a potato. These form the participants' instruction sheets.
3.   Hand one instruction sheet and a pencil to each participant. Remember to shuffle the sheets of paper if you are handing them out to participants sitting in a circle otherwise they will already be arranged in the chain's order.
4.   Ask the participants to find the second item on the paper by first introducing themselves 'I am John Smith' and then asking each other 'are you a potato?' or whatever article they are seeking.
5.   If the answer is 'no' the participants find someone else to ask.
6.   If the answer is 'yes, I am a potato' that person who has been asked adds, 'find a telephone' or whatever the second article is on their slip.
7.   When a participant finds an item they write it down on their sheet of paper.
8.   The exercise continues until a participant completes the chain in the correct order. That is, they are told to find themselves.

Review   None.

Variations The personal introductions can be extended to include telling other participants something memorable about themselves or their role.

2 Cooperative Tower

Description   The participants each have a piece (or pieces) of a tower that matches those required to construct a replica of an already constructed tower.

Purpose   This approach to group introductions takes us into problem solving immediately. Energy levels are raised from the outset.

Materials   Lego® or similar plastic construction pieces.

Duration   About 15 minutes depending on the number of participants and the complexity of the tower to be copied.

Procedure
1. Build a tower using at least 20 construction pieces. Include a variety of colours and sizes.
2. Put an identical set of tower pieces in a plastic bag.
3. Calculate how many pieces each participant must take from the bag. Some participants may have more pieces than others, for example, for 12 participants building a 20 piece tower; 8 participants will have 2 pieces and 4 participants 1 piece each.
4. As participants arrive (or once they have all assembled) ask them to take a piece (or pieces) from the bag.
5. Reveal the tower and ask the participants to introduce themselves to each other and using the pieces they each have replicate the tower on display.

Review   Discuss how the group went about solving the problem and the effect a new team has on performance.

Variations   For a large group needing to be broken down into a number of teams, construct a number of towers equal to the number of teams required. These may be smaller towers than for the exercise previously described. You may opt for unique towers or have some pieces duplicated, which can add some interesting dynamics. Each participant picks one piece from the bag. The towers are then built and the participant joins the team where their piece was used as a part of the construction.

3   Coupled

Description   This is a quick way for participants to talk to each other and to arrange themselves into pairs.

Purpose   This exercise provides an alternative and energetic approach to introductions within the group.

Materials   Prepared cards (preferable) or a list.

Duration   10 minutes, depending on the number of participants.

Procedure
1. Prepare a set of paired items, for example, needle and cotton, hammer and nail, Romeo and Juliet, etc.
2. Issue a card to participants (or tell them what they are from the list).
3. Ask them to think of one memorable thing about themselves and decide what or who might be their partner.
4. Ask them to find their partner, using the following approach outlined below.
5. Whilst searching for their partner they should say the following to each person they meet 'Good morning/afternoon/evening. My name is X, the memorable thing about me is ..., and I am looking for Y (for example, Cotton)'. Note: They should not say what is on their card only who or what they believe their partner is.
6. Once coupled the pair seeks out other couples where they have not met one or both of that pair previously. When couples meet they introduce the other member of their couple in turn by saying 'Good morning/afternoon/evening. This is X, they are memorable because of ... and we are A and B (for examplè, Needle and Cotton)'.
7. Once everybody has met sit the group in a circle and for each individual ask the other group members (apart from their partner) the person's name and why they are memorable.

Review   Discuss having something memorable to say about yourself as an aid to being remembered.

Variations   None.

4   Dominoes

Description The participants are each given a domino (or dominoes) as they arrive to help to facilitate introductions and to solve the problem of creating the longest domino chain(s). It is best used for groups of 14 or more people.

Purpose This is an energizing ice breaker that facilitates the opening introductions. It looks a straightforward exercise but there are many combinations to be considered when trying to create a long chain.

Materials A set of dominoes. (or make a set using index cards).

Duration 10 minutes.

Procedure
1. Give each participant one or two dominoes.
2. Ask the participants to make the longest possible domino chain.
3. The participants with two dominoes can only 'play' one of their dominoes. They may change the one they are 'playing' at any point in the exercise. For example, if a person held 5/3 and 4/2 they may choose to be 5/3 initially but may later change to 4/2 if that helped produce a longer chain.
4. Ask the participants to find the other(s) with whom they can form a chain.
5. When participants meet they shake hands and exchange names and the value of their dominoes.
6. If the participants have two values the same, for example, 5/4 and

4/3 they may 'link' and look for participants who have available either a 5 or 3 on their domino.

7. If they do not have values on their dominoes that match, the participants will move on to meet another participant or chain of participants and repeat steps 5 and 6.

8. Participants may break and reform the chains' order as often as necessary whilst attempting to create a long chain. Whenever a participant changes places they will shake hands and exchange names with their new link.

Review   Discuss how the group approached solving the problem. Did the problem solving hinder name retention?

Variations   Children's picture domino cards can make the exercise even more fun.

5 First Impressions

Description Participants record the first impression they have of each other. The exercise works best with more than 10 participants.

Purpose First impressions are extremely important in business and this ice breaker may provide valuable feedback to participants.

Materials Pencil, A4 sheet of paper and something to rest on while writing, for example, a book or clip board, for each participant.
Masking tape or safety pins.

Duration About 20 minutes, but this will vary according to the number of participants.

Procedure
1. Give each participant a sheet of paper, a pencil, some tape or a safety pin.
2. Ask the participants to form a circle and fix the A4 sheet of paper onto the back of the person on their right, using the masking tape or safety pin.
3. Ask the group to walk around and introduce themselves to each other. The participants should have a short conversation about their role and/or say something memorable about themselves.
4. At the end of the conversation each participant writes **at the bottom** of the sheet of paper a short first impression, using no more than five words, and initial their comment. The paper is then folded over so that the other participants cannot see the comment. Note: The first impression should be honest and blatant insults should be avoided.
5. Steps 3 and 4 are repeated until everybody has met one another or about 10–12 minutes have elapsed.
6. Participants return to the circle and the person on their right removes the folded first impression sheet.
7. Introductions are then completed by each participant introducing the person on their left by saying 'This is John Smith and our first impressions were (read from the sheet of paper)'.

Review Discuss the importance of first impressions and be prepared to explore in greater depth anything that has come as a complete surprise to any participants. If necessary a separate 'off line' session may be run.
Note: Participants are asked to initial their impressions to reduce the likelihood of inappropriate comment and recipients expending energy trying to identify who made particular comments.

Variations
1. It can be run at the end of an event but called Lasting Impressions.
2. After the main session the group can break up into teams of about four people to discuss the comments made about each individual.

6   In a Spin

Description   The participants spin the plate and have to call out another participant's name. Can be used at the start of day two of an event.

Purpose   An energizing ice breaker which could be run on the second day to re-inforce remembering participants' names.

Materials   An unbreakable plate.
A table if it is difficult for participants to bend down to ground level easily.

Duration   5 minutes.

Procedure
1. If the participants have not already been introduced have a brief introduction session (not included in timing).
2. Start by spinning the plate on the floor or tabletop and calling out another participant's name.
3. You may not call the name of the person who called you or, once the exercise is under way, the name of the person who called them.
4. On hearing your name called you go to the plate and keep it spinning.
5. Repeat steps 2 and 3.
6. A participant is disqualified if they cannot remember a name or if they call out an invalid name.
7. The exercise stops once everybody has had a turn at spinning the plate or after five minutes, that is, before the novelty wears off.

Review   Not necessary

Variations   None.

7 Job Mime

Description   The participants mime to each other their job or role.

Purpose   This activity is an energetic ice breaker that incorporates some creativity.

Materials   A whistle. If you do not have a whistle use some other 'time out' mechanism.

Duration   About 20 –30 minutes, depending on the size of the group.

Procedure
1. Ask participants to think of a mime that describes their job or role. Allow three minutes for this phase.
2. Ask participants to walk round the room and, as they meet someone, to shake hands and exchange names.
3. This continues for three or four exchanges and then the leader blows the whistle.
4. On hearing the whistle each pair not only exchanges names but also mimes the role. They will have to decide who mimes first.
5. The person not miming has to guess the job or role of the other. They may ask questions to help them guess the other person's role.
6. The person miming must only answer 'Yes' or 'No' to the questions.
7. After 90 seconds blow the whistle. If the role has not been guessed the person miming tells their partner what their job or role is.
8. After 30 seconds blow the whistle and the other member of the pair mimes their role. Steps 5 to 7 are then repeated.
9. After both have mimed their role each moves on to find a new partner. Steps 2 to 8 are repeated.
10. The exercise continues for about 20 minutes or until everybody has mimed to one another. It is best to let the energy levels determine the timings.

Review   Discuss precision questioning techniques used to help identify the mimed role.

Variations   Individual mimes are made to the whole group, which is allowed 10 questions to guess the role.

8   Matchmakers

Description	Participants introduce themselves and try to win matches.
Purpose	An energizing introduction exercise with an added edge. The exercise works best with 10 or more people.
Materials	Matchsticks. A large bag of them can be obtained from a craft shop.
Duration	10 minutes.
Procedure	1. Give each participant 10 matches. 2. Ask each person to put some of their matches in their right hand and then hold their clenched fist slightly in front of themselves. They should take care that the others do not observe them. 3. Ask people to circulate and on meeting each other decide who will go first. The participant going first says 'I am John Smith, odd or even?' 4. The other participant guesses whether there is an odd or even number of matchsticks in the clenched fist. 5. The first participant opens their hand and if the other participant has guessed correctly they take one match. 6. The roles are then reversed with the second participant giving their name and asking 'odd or even?' 7. If their partner guesses correctly they take a match and the transaction between them is complete. 8. Each participant begins circulating again looking for a new partner. 9. The exercise continues until someone has no matches or after seven minutes, whichever is the sooner.
Review	Not necessary.
Variations	None.

9   Name Game

Description   The participants introduce themselves to each other as they attempt to solve an anagram.

Purpose   This is an ice breaker and simple puzzle solving exercise that provides an alternative to conventional introductions.

Materials   A pencil and paper for each participant.
A prepared card or paper for each participant.
Masking tape or safety pins.
Remove any mirrors from the room.

Duration   30 minutes.

Procedure   1. Decide on a set of names containing the same number of letters, about 8–10 letters long. If possible use names that are relevant to the event.
2. Prepare a card or piece of paper for each participant with the appropriate name written on it.
3. Attach a card to the back of each person and say how many letters there are in the name.
4. Ask the participants to discover the name stuck to their back by asking fellow players about the letters on the card.
5. Ask the participants to circulate and when two meet they introduce themselves to each other and then inquire about the letters on their card, for example, 'Do I have an E?' If the answer is yes they write the 'E' down. Note: If there are two letters the same only one may be revealed at a time.
6. Consecutive questions are not allowed and having written down the letter the participants then move on to meet someone else and repeat the process.
7. Having found all the letters the participants try to solve the anagram.

Review   Not necessary.

Variations   None.

10   Recipe for Success

Description   Participants introduce themselves to each other while they determine for which 'Dish of the Day' they are an ingredient.

Purpose   An ice breaker that can also be used as a method of team selection.

Materials   A recipe book to prepare ingredient cards or list.

Duration   About 10 minutes, depending on number of participants.

Procedure
1. From the recipe book select three or more dishes whose total ingredient list equals the number of participants. Avoid using a common ingredient.
2. Write each ingredient on a card or list.
3. Give a card to each participant or tell them their ingredient individually.
4. Ask the participants to find the other ingredients with which they should be combined to make a 'Dish of the Day'. Tell them the names of the 'Dishes of the Day' they are expected to be able to create.
5. As they meet, participants should shake hands and tell each other their name as well as their ingredient.
6. When a set of ingredients has come together the group must agree which 'Dish of the Day' they constitute.

Review   Discuss the process the participants employed to determine the dishes.

Variations
1. Do not give the names of the dishes, but be prepared for some unusual suggested dishes.
2. Make a meal of it comprising a Starter, Main Course, Dessert, and so on depending on the number of the teams.

11 Rogue's Gallery

Description Participants draw a self portrait, but using the 'wrong' hand.

Purpose The exercise is intended to be a humorous energizing aid to facilitate introductions.

Materials Pencil and A4 paper for each participant.
Tables, or something for each person to rest their paper on.

Duration 15 minutes.

Procedure
1. Distribute the pencils and paper and ask participants, if possible, to locate themselves where they cannot observe each other's work. Alternatively, they promise not to look at their neighbour's work.
2. Tell the participants that they have 5 minutes to draw a caricature of themselves using the hand they do not normally write with.
3. Ask the participants to think of three memorable facts about themselves while they are drawing.
4. At the end of the exercise collect all the pictures, label them A, B, C, and so on, and display them for the group to see.
5. Select each self portrait in turn and ask the group to identify the artist. Alternatively the group can work as individuals and using a pencil and paper match the faces to the participants.
6. After each caricature has been identified ask the artist to declare themselves and to tell the group three memorable facts about themselves.

Review Discuss how people recognized the artists and the role of using memorable incidents to help people remember you.

Variation The exercise can be undertaken using the 'right' hand, but is less fun and gives those participants with artistic skills too much of an advantage.

12   Round the Ring

Description   The participants exchange their name and three memorable facts about themselves.

Purpose   This is an alternative to conventional, and often boring, introductions around the group.

Materials   None.

Duration   About 30 minutes, depending on the number of participants.

Procedure
1. Ask all the participants to think of three memorable facts about themselves. Allow about 3 minutes for this part of the exercise.
2. Split the group in half. If there is an odd number a trainer or co-trainer should join in to make up the numbers.
3. Ask one half of the group to form a large circle (large enough to reduce noise interference between members in the circle) facing outward.
4. Ask the members of the other half of the group to face a person forming the circle, that is, they form an outer circle facing inward.
5. Tell the pairs facing each other that they have one minute to shake hands and to exchange names together with the three memorable facts about themselves.
6. Having exchanged the information the outer circle moves round one place clockwise.
7. The new pair then has one minute to shake hands and exchange information.
8. This process continues until the other circle returns to the person they first met. The start point.
9. On returning to the start point, each one of the pair tells their partner their partner's name and the three memorable facts about their partner.
10. If they are wrong or cannot remember, the partner corrects them.
11. Having exchanged this information the members of the outer circle move round one place clockwise and repeat the exchange process.
12. This continues until the members of the outer circle return to their start point.
13. The group then forms a large circle.
14. Select a participant at random and the rest of the group (the half who know) supply the name and memorable points of the person selected.

15. This can be repeated until all the participants have been selected. You should make the selections quickly and require quick responses from the group to inject pace and energy into the proceedings.

Review Lead a discussion on how people remember names and the memorable information. Also discuss how memorable information can help people remember you.

Variations None.

13   Who is it?

Description   The participants must find out as much as possible about each other and identify specific individuals from a list of facts.

Purpose   This is an alternative and energizing way to conduct introductions instead of a round robin approach, which can often result in boredom.

Materials   None.

Duration   30–40 minutes.

Procedure
1. Tell the participants that they are required to find out as much about each other as they can during a 15-minute period.
2. Ask the participants to circulate, introduce themselves to each other and engage in short conversations aimed at eliciting as much information as possible. Note: Participants should aim to have about five conversations during this phase.
3. Ask the participants to sit in a horseshoe or circle formation.
4. Select a participant at random from the circle and ask them to describe another member of the group from the facts they collected during their conversation with them.
5. The remaining members of the group attempt to identify who is being described. But they cannot name themselves.
6. If no one can identify the description the describer then indicates whom they have described.
7. Whoever has been described then describes another member of the group.
8. Steps 5 to 8 are repeated until everybody in the group has been described.

Review   Discuss the strategies that might be used to capture key information about individuals, particularly in social situations.

Variations   None.

14   Who's Next?

Description   The participants must remember quickly each other's names.

Purpose   This is an ice breaker that can also be used on day two of an event to reinforce earlier name learning.

Materials   None.

Duration   10–15 minutes.

Procedure
1. Seat participants and leader in a circle or horseshoe.
2. Ask participants to briefly introduce or, if it is day two, re-introduce themselves.
3. Start the exercise by pointing at one of the participants and asking, 'Who's next?'
4. If you point with your right hand, the participant who is being pointed at must immediately call out the name of the person on their right; if you point with your left hand, the participant must give the name of the person on their left.
5. The person who has been pointed at then repeats the process by pointing at another participant using the same right and left rules.
6. Let the exercise run for a couple of minutes for the names to register; then increase the pace and introduce the rule that any participant going in the wrong direction or forgetting a name is disqualified.

Review   Not necessary.

Variations
1. Halfway through, introduce the rule that pointing with the right hand means name the person on the left and pointing with the left hand means name the person on the right.
2. Add yet another level of complexity by making the right/left rules change with each go. For example: Go 1. Right hand = person on right. Go 2. Right hand = person on left. Go 3. Right hand = person on right, and so on.

II

Team and Small Group Exercises

Today much of our work is conducted as a team. This is nothing new; we learned many millennia ago that to survive, teamwork is essential, for without it a community might starve. Its members needed to cooperate, particularly when hunting, for if they did not they might easily become the meal. Today's corporations also wish to avoid being eaten and teamwork is crucial to their ability to function successfully. Much of my time as a consultant is spent helping individual team members work more effectively together and the organization's teams to work in harmony towards common goals. Almost all of this hinges on people's behaviours and communication.

In my book *How to Deliver Training*[1] I note that much training is conducted within groups, often because it reflects the way we work in our organizations. However, learning within groups introduces a dynamic that must be allowed for when designing a training event. The main feature is that the trainer must consider both the social/maintenance and task dimensions of group work. Team and small group exercises can often help advance the group's development or provide insights into its current state. Frequently it is the discussions following on from an exercise, sometimes in the bar or over dinner, that reveal the real team learning or development nuggets. You have to keep on panning.

[1]Orridge, M. *How to Deliver Training*, Gower, 1998.

15 Bombard the Balloon

Description   Opposing teams of 6–12 members bombard a balloon with newspaper paper balls with the object of rolling the balloon over their opponent's line to score a goal.

Purpose   Competitive energizer to liven up an otherwise 'heavy' session.

Materials   A round blown up balloon – have some spare ones available.
24 sheets of newspaper, each rolled up into a ball.
Masking tape.

Duration   10 minutes.

Procedure
1.   Screw up the 24 sheets of newspaper to form 24 balls.
2.   Determine the number and size of teams – between 6 and 12 to a team.
3.   Give the teams twelve paper balls each.
4.   Using the masking tape lay out the 'pitch' with four parallel lines 4 metres and 6 metres apart as indicated. Mark the centre of the pitch.

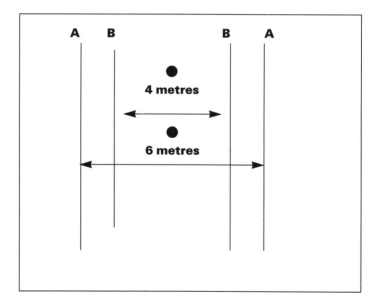

5.   Each team stands in a line behind line A. They must not throw a ball or touch the balloon in front of the line.
6.   The balloon is placed on the centre spot.

7. At the start signal each team pelts the balloon with their paper balls trying to get the balloon over their opponent's line B and score a goal.
8. Balls from the opposing team may be retrieved and re-used.
9. If a goal is scored the balls are shared out again.
10. The next game is started.

Review   Not necessary.

Variation   Allow 3 minutes a game or the first team who scores 5 goals wins.

16 Candle Power

Description Two teams of 8–10 persons compete to blow out their own candle but not their opponents'. The exercise requires even numbers in the team, unless one member has two turns.

Purpose Energizing team competitive exercise that involves communication and trust.

Materials Two blindfolds, one for each team.
Two candles – use two different colours or mark the candles so that they are distinguishable.
A table.
Matches or a cigarette lighter.

Duration 15 minutes.

Procedure
1. Place the table in the centre of the room.
2. Place two lighted candles on the table about 0.25 metres apart and tell the teams which is their candle. **Safety note:** Position yourself by the table to ensure that no one singes themselves during the exercise.
3. Position the teams at either end of the room about 3 metres from the table. Note: Diagonally opposite corners of the room can provide extra distance.
4. Ask the teams to decide team member order.
5. Explain that the object of the exercise is to blow out the team's candle while not blowing out the opponents'. The problem is that the person trying to blow out the candle will be blindfold and instructions will be provided by another team member.
6. The first player in each team is blindfolded and is then carefully spun round by the second player three times.
7. Start the exercise, the first players then make their way towards the table and have to blow out their candle only. The first person to blow out the candle wins.
8. If the wrong candle, that is, the opponents' candle, is blown out then the other team wins.
9. Instructions can be issued to the blindfolded player by the next one in line, who can position themselves to have a good view of the table from their end of the room, but only seven words may be used – Stop, Go, Left, Right, Up, Down, and Blow.
10. After the candle has been blown out re-light it so that the remaining team members can attempt the challenge in turn.

11. The winning team is the one with the greatest number of successful blows.

Review   Explore how the blindfolded person felt, the issuing of instructions and the effect of noise on completing the exercise.

Variation   Instead of candles the players can carry sand on a large spoon and have to empty it into a plastic cup. Change the 'blow' command to 'tip'. After all have played, the team with the most sand in the cup wins.

17   Carry On Carrying

Description   Team members carry each other using a variety of different methods. Teams of at least six people will create the best dynamics.

Purpose   Team energizing activity, which requires creativity to think of original ways to transport team members.

Materials   Masking tape.
A chair, or similar marker, for example, a traffic cone, for each team.

Duration   10 minutes.

Procedure   1.   Organize the group into teams of six or more participants. Note: You must issue the following or similar instruction 'People with back problems, hernias or who should avoid lifting should not take part in this exercise'.

2.   Teams should organize themselves into approximate weight/ height/strength order. Note: You may wish to omit this instruction to the teams to see if they take account of these factors when organizing themselves.

3.   Using masking tape mark the starting point for each team.

4.   Position each team's chair about 3 metres away from the masking tape start line. Allow at least 1.5 metres between the chairs.

5.   Tell the teams that they have to carry their fellow team members from the start line, round the chair and back to the start/finish line.

6.   The first team member carries the second member of the team, the second carries the third and so on until the last member of the team has been carried by the next to last team member.

7.   The method of transport may not be repeated. For example, if the first method is a piggyback, no one else in the team can use the piggyback method.

8.   If a team member being carried touches the floor the pair return to the start line and re-start their attempt.

9.   Give the teams 90 seconds to organize themselves.

10.   Begin the exercise.

11.   The first team to complete the exercise is declared the winner.

Review   Discuss how the teams organized themselves to undertake the exercise, particularly concerning size and weight.

Variations   None.

18   Celebrity Island

Description   Individual team members choose a celebrity, book, and object to be stranded with on a desert island. The team prioritizes their individual choices to form a subset that the team would like on their island.

Purpose   The exercise allows for individual creativity in determining what they would take to the island followed by a group decision making/consensus phase that will help develop the team dynamics.

Materials   Pencil and paper for each individual.
Flip chart and pen per team.

Duration   About 45 minutes, depending on the number of teams.

Procedure   1.   In the plenary session tell the participants that they have five minutes to decide which celebrity, book, and object they would wish to be stranded with on a desert island.
2.   After five minutes the participants form teams of four to six people (if they are not already allocated to a team for the event).
3.   Tell the teams that they have 25 minutes to select from each individual's list the three celebrities, books, and objects that they wish to have on their desert island.

4. The selections and reasons for each choice will be recorded on a flip chart.
5. After 25 minutes the teams return to the plenary session and present their choices and reasoning.

Review   Discuss how the teams decided on their choices. What were the decision criteria? How was consensus achieved? How did individuals feel about the process?

Variation   When the teams return to the plenary group a representative from each team is required to negotiate and to agree in 10 minutes the three celebrities, books, and objects the whole group should have on the desert island. Other members observe the negotiation process, which is discussed at the end of the exercise.

19   Centipede Run

Description   Teams of five or more players crouch down to form themselves into a centipede, and race.

Purpose   Large group energizing activity.

Materials   None.
A room at least 6 metres long is required, alternatively the exercise can be conducted outdoors.
A chair per team – optional.

Duration   5 minutes.

Procedure
1. Divide the group into teams of five or more players.
2. Form them into lines at the end of the room.
3. Team members squat on their heels and place their hands on the shoulders or waist of the person in front of them.
4. Give the signal to start the race
5. The centipedes move forward by walking, not hopping or bouncing.
6. When they reach the far end of the room (or chair) the centipede must turn and head back towards the start/finish line.
7. If at any time in the race a player loses contact with the person in front, that team must stop and reconnect.
8. To do this the tail of the centipede must stop while the front end goes back to join it.

Review   Not necessary but you can lead a discussion on team working and communication.

Variation   Tell participants to bounce along instead of walking.

20   Cup Tower Relay

Description   Teams build a tower of paper cups and plates in relay. Between five and eight team members works best.

Purpose   This is a team energizing activity.

Materials   One paper cup and one paper plate per team member. Disposable plastic cups may be used as an alternative to paper cups.
A table for each team.
A chair for each team.

Duration   10 minutes.

Procedure   1.   Place the team table and chair about 6 metres apart.
2.   Put the teams' plates and cups on the team tables – a plate and cup per team member.

3. Ask the team members to form a line behind their table. Issue the remaining instructions.
4. On the word 'Go' the first team member picks up a plate and places a paper cup on it.
5. Balancing the cup on the plate, which is held in one hand, the member goes down the room, round the chair and back towards their table. Only the plate may be held while navigating the course.
6. While the first team member is going down the room the second in line also balances a cup on a paper plate.
7. When the first person returns to the table he or she places their cup and plate on the second person's cup and plate.
8. The second team member then sets off down the course.
9. The cup-tower becomes higher with each successive hand-over. The exercise continues until the last team member has completed the course.
10. If the tower collapses, or a player uses the other hand to steady it, he or she must go back to the table, rebuild the tower and start the lap again.
11. The first team to complete the exercise is the winner.

Review   Lead a discussion on strategy and the pressure on the latter team members.

Variation   Have a large supply of plates and cups and continue the exercise for a set time, say 5 minutes, and the team with the tallest tower when 'time out' is called is declared the winner.

21   Diabolical Dialogue

Description   Teams are given three lines of dialogue that they must incorporate into a short play.

Purpose   This can be used purely as an energizer but may also allow the exploration of team dynamics and creativity.

Materials   A pencil and paper for each participant.

Duration   30 minutes.

Procedure
1. Organize the group into teams of three to five members.
2. Give pencil and paper to all the members of the group and request them to make up and write one line of dialogue on their paper.
3. Collect the sheets of paper and fold them so that the words cannot be seen.
4. Allow each team to choose three pieces of folded paper.
5. Tell the teams that they have 10 minutes to build a 'playlet' that incorporates the three pieces of dialogue.
6. The teams take it in turns to perform their plays.
7. At the end of each 'playlet' the other members of the group, with the exception of those who wrote the dialogue, guess which were the three chosen lines of dialogue.

Review   Discuss how the teams worked on their performances.

Variation   For a greater challenge the first piece of dialogue should be used at the beginning of the 'playlet', the second piece in the middle and the third piece at the end.

22   Fire! Fire!

Description   A small group exercise where the team decides which six objects it would rescue from a fire at the training/event venue, and give reasons, preferably humorous.

Purpose   A short energizing creative exercise.

Materials   Flip chart and pen per team.

Duration   15 minutes.

Procedure
1. Request the teams to identify six items they would rescue in the event of the training location catching fire, and to give a reason for each.
2. After 10 minutes the teams present their choices to each other.

Review   An exploration of the teams' decision-making processes may be revealing.

Variation   Substitute flood or earthquake for fire.

23   Freeze Frame

Description   Each team, of between three and six members, produces an improvisation using allocated roles. Having developed the role play the teams 'freeze frame' one scene from the improvisation from which another team have to decide what is happening at that time, what led up to the freeze frame, and how the scene was concluded. The improvisation is then acted out in its entirety.

Purpose   This develops not only team and individual creativity but also feeds into a discussion on the assumptions made and conclusions drawn from limited information.

Materials   None, though teams may find appropriate props to help them with their improvisation.

Duration   45–60 minutes depending on the number of teams.

Procedure
1. Prepare a list of characters for each team. Use a complete range of organizational roles and for some teams include other stakeholders like customers and suppliers. For example, Team 1 may have a CEO (Chief Executive Officer), Personnel Director, Trade Union Representative, Secretary, Clerical Assistant, and Teamaker, whereas Team 2 may have a CEO, Salesperson, Customer, Secretary, Storekeeper, and Lorry Driver.
2. Allocate the pre-determined roles to the teams and tell each team that they have 25 minutes to develop a 5-minute improvisation depicting a business incident of their choice.
3. Tell the teams that having developed the improvisation they should decide which scene, from somewhere near the middle of the improvisation, will be 'freeze framed'.
4. The teams produce their improvisation and 'freeze frame'.
5. The performance order is agreed.
6. The first team sets up its 'freeze frame' and the other teams suggest what is happening in the frozen scene, what led up to it and how it was concluded.
7. The freeze frame team then acts out their improvisation, briefly freezing at the freeze frame point of the play.
8. The process is repeated for each team.

Review   The review may take two forms. The first can examine the creativity employed in producing the improvisation and the second can examine the assumptions we make and conclusions we draw from the limited information provided by the freeze frame. There are a number of areas which can be explored like culture, previous experiences, and personal prejudices.

Variation   Provide each team with an incident they are to depict and they choose their own characters. The teams must not know each other's incident.

24 Hilarious History

Description   Team members must invent a story that incorporates historical characters in an unusual and amusing way. Three to five members in the team.

Purpose   Team creativity warm up exercise.

Materials   Pencil and paper per team.
Flip chart and pen (optional).

Duration   20 minutes.

Procedure   1. Ask the teams' members to take it in turn to suggest eight (teams of
three or four members) or ten (teams with five members) historical
characters.
2. These are recorded (a flip chart may be used).
3. Tell the teams they have 15 minutes to compose and write down a
story which incorporates all the characters they have selected. The
funnier the better.
4. After the allotted time the teams return to a plenary session and read
out their stories.

Review   The review may be part of a general discussion on creativity. Team working may also be explored.

Variations   None.

25 Hole in One

Description The participants design a 'tool' to load balls into cups.

Purpose This is a team building and problem solving exercise requiring cooperation and creativity.

Materials Give the following identical materials to each team.

Three table tennis balls.
A disposable plastic cup per team for use during the practice phase.
10 disposable cups for competition phase.
A 1.5–2.0 metre long table.
A chair.
Paper or newspaper, for example, two sheets of flip chart paper or two copies of a broadsheet newspaper.
Card.
Paper clips.
A stapler and staples.
Adhesive tape.
4 metres of parcel string.

For the competition phase:

20 table tennis balls.
A clock or watch for time keeping.

Duration 45 minutes.

Procedure For each team place a disposable cup at one end of the table and a chair at the far end as shown below.

1. Give each team the materials with the instruction to construct a 'tool' that will enable a table tennis ball to be remotely loaded from the far end of the table into the cup. There are two key team roles when loading takes place, the 'aimer' and 'loader'. The 'aimer' indicates to the 'loader' where to position the tool to allow a ball to be correctly

deposited into the cup. During loading the following rules must also be observed:

- Only one member of the team, the 'aimer' is allowed beyond the chair end of the table.
- No members of the team can touch the table while loading is in progress.
- The chair must be sat on by the 'loader' while loading is in progress.

2. Describe the competition phase to the teams (steps 4 and 5).
3. The teams have 30 minutes to construct and test their loading tool.
4. After 30 minutes the competition phase commences. Each team has 30 seconds to load the cups using their 'tool' and to score as many points as possible. The table will be arranged as follows:

Points are awarded as follows:
Front row – 1 point
Second row – 2 points
Third row – 3 points
Back row – 5 points

5. The winning team is the one to score the highest number of points. Note: Have about 20 table tennis balls available for this phase.

Review   Discuss the teams' problem solving approach, roles, and the strategy adopted to solve the problem.

Variations   None.

26 Hot Air Balloon

Description   Team members choose three famous people to travel together in a balloon. They then decide which of these people should be sacrificed, by being jettisoned overboard, when the balloon springs a leak. Team sizes of three to five work best in this exercise.

Purpose   This exercise concentrates on team decision making and achieving a consensus.

Materials   A pencil and paper for each participant.

Duration   45 minutes.

Procedure   *Phase 1 – Allow 10 minutes.*

1. Organize the large group into teams of three to five.
2. Ask each team member to think of a person they admire. The person can be living or dead.
3. The team members think about and then note down some of the key points behind their choice of person.

Phase 2 – Allow 35 minutes.

1. Tell them that the people the team members have chosen are travelling together in a balloon and that the balloon has sprung a leak.
2. The team members then have to decide which one has to be sacrificed to save the others.
3. Having made their decisions the teams meet in the plenary group and indicate who were the balloon's occupants and which one of them was sacrificed.

Review   Explore in the plenary session how the teams arrived at consensus paying particular attention to how individuals felt about the decision.

Variation   Have pre-selected historical figures to choose from. This lessens the personal identification with the balloon's occupants. Note: You may wish to have some notes prepared summarizing their achievements or notoriety.

27   House of Cards

Description   The teams construct a tower using playing cards; but they may also gamble for more materials. The ideal team size for this exercise is three. Teams of five or more will probably be too large.

Purpose   The exercise introduces overt risk-taking as well as the usual teamworking and problem solving aspects of traditional tower building approaches.

Materials   Two packs of playing cards for each team. Have a different design for each team.
A spare pack of playing cards for each team, held by the dealer.
Two packs of cards to be used for gambling held by the 'dealer'. These should also be of a different design.
A table for each team and an additional 'gambling' table. If possible put a cloth on the tables to increase friction and the towers' stability.
A tape measure or rule.
A trainer will need to act as dealer.

Duration   15 minutes.

Procedure   1.   Give each team two packs of cards – have different designs or colours for each team.

2. Tell the teams that the object of the exercise is to build the tallest house of cards.
3. Tell the teams that gambling for additional building materials is allowed.
4. Once the exercise has started a team member may bring any number of cards to a maximum of one pack to attempt to win more building materials.
5. The gambling house rules are as follows:

- A participant wishing to gamble tells the dealer how many cards he or she wishes to gamble. The participant lays that number of cards on the table.
- The dealer deals, face down, the same number of cards the team member is prepared to gamble into a pile in front of that player. The dealer deals himself the same number of cards.
- Each of them then takes a card from the top of their pile and turns it over to show the value.
- Whoever has the higher number wins those cards, but if the values are the same then another card is turned over by each until there is a winner of the cards played.
- The game continues until all cards in the pile have been played.
- The dealer then reckons up and either takes cards from the player or gives extra cards equivalent to the winnings.
- If more than one team wish to play at the same time then the game becomes three or more handed.
- Note: The dealer's cards are used for the game to prevent unscrupulous players bringing only high value cards with which to gamble.

6. The winning team is the one that builds the tallest tower in 15 minutes.

Review   Discuss the teams' strategy and why they decided or not to gamble. What pressures, if any, were on the builder and gambler? How did they feel when they succeeded or failed in their respective roles? Did they change roles during the exercise?

Variations   None.

28   Mini Assault Course

Description   The team must negotiate itself and its 'treasure' through a string assault course. This can be held indoors or (preferable) outdoors.

Purpose   Team problem solving exercise which requires cooperation between all team members.

Materials   One cup with handle, preferably plastic, for each team member.
A blindfold for each team member.
Water and measuring container.
20+ metres of string.
 If held indoors use chairs as obstacles.

Duration   A maximum of 10 minutes for each team.

Procedure
1. In advance prepare a string trail through bushes, etc. (or use chairs if indoors) threading one end of the string through the cup handles. Tie off the string at each end. To ensure that the cup handle does not become fouled or snagged put large loops in the string trail so there is some slack for going around the obstacles.
2. Test that it is possible for a cup to be taken from one end of the course to the other.
3. Assemble a team at the start of the trail, fill their cups to within approximately 1.25 cm of the top and record the water used.
4. Blindfold each team member.
5. The team members are required to reach the other end of the course without spilling any water.
6. On completing the course measure the water in the cups.
7. The winning team is the one which completes the course with the most water within the prescribed time limit (10 minutes or whatever has been set). In the event of a tie the fastest team is the winner.

Note: To save time, provided it is still fair, the next team can attempt the course in the reverse order.

Review   Discuss how the team communicated, particularly when facing obstacles.

Variation   Have two similar string courses over which two teams race. Each team has a team leader, who is not part of the blindfolded team, giving instructions.

29   New Similes

Description   The teams are required to find some everyday objects from around the venue and construct similes based on them.

Purpose   The exercise focuses on developing team creativity.

Materials   A button or similar everyday object that forms the basis of a well-known simile.
Pencil and paper or flip chart and pen for each team.

Duration   15 minutes.

Procedure   1. In the plenary session show the button or other chosen object and ask what simile it reminds the participants of. For example 'As bright as a button'.
2. Ask each team to find six items at the venue and then construct a simile based on each item.
3. The similes are recorded using the paper or flip chart.
4. The teams return to the plenary session and take it in turns to read out a simile.

Review   Discuss the role of similes in helping limber up from a creative problem solving exercise.

Variation   With fewer than six participants the exercise can be conducted individually with each individual creating four similes.

30   Newspaper List

Description   Teams of up to four people must make up a sentence using words selected from a page of a newspaper.

Purpose   The exercise may be used as a creative team energizer in support of team building and team problem solving.

Materials   Newspaper – a page for each team. Use pages with solid text if possible. Pencil and paper or flip chart and pen for each team.

Duration   15 minutes.

Procedure
1. Give each team a page from a newspaper.
2. Starting at the top of the first column ask the teams to find the first word beginning with A.
3. The word is circled and noted down on the paper or flip chart.
4. Ask the teams to continue the process all the way through the alphabet. The first word beginning with B, then C, and so on excluding the letters X and Z.
5. The teams have five minutes to search for the words.
6. Each team should have 24 words There may be occasions when there are some missing words and a second page will be required to produce 24 words.
7. Give the teams five minutes to make the longest reasonably sensible sentence from the words they have found.
8. The teams return to the plenary session and read out their offerings.

Review   Team dynamics and processes may be reviewed at the end of the plenary session.

Variation   The exercise may be undertaken by individuals rather than teams.

31 Picture It

Description   Team members use themselves to build a picture or series of pictures to reflect a scene or business situation.

Purpose   The exercise allows for team creativity and cooperation in exploring either general or specific business situations.

Materials   None.

Duration   10 minutes plus 5 minutes discussion per picture.

Procedure   1. Give each team the title of a scene you wish them to depict. Examples might be 'The Angry Customer', 'Winning the Order', 'Fraud', 'Workplace Bullying', 'My First Day', or more general ones like 'War', 'Commuting', 'A Picnic'.
2. The team members jointly imagine they are creating a scene to be photographed.
3. Each team has seven minutes to design a picture.
4. Each team takes it in turns to show the picture to the large group.
5. Once in position the *whole* group, facilitated by the leader, discusses the picture and the reasons behind the various images depicted.

Review   A review is built into the procedure but an additional one can be held to explore the team process.

Variation   Give each team one element of a topical situation to depict. An example might be

Customer returns faulty goods

Customer demands to see manager

Customer argues with manager

Customer is satisfied/dissatisfied with outcome

The group may discuss precisely what happened to cause and resolve the situation in each of their pictures.

32 Pond Life

Description The participants design an environmentally balanced system.

Purpose This approach can be used as a metaphor for an organization and allows participants to explore cause and effect.

Materials A prepared sheet of flip chart paper for each team showing the cross section of a lake which should include shallow and deep water. Just for fun, you may wish to show a supermarket trolley or rubbish dumped in the lake.
Flip chart and pens.

Duration 15–20 minutes.

Procedure
1. Tell the team members that you have decided to retire and set up a fishing lake. Your goal is to have it in total environmental balance and therefore maintenance free.
2. Each team has 10 minutes to construct, by drawing, a balanced system for the fishing lake that meets your goal.
3. The teams present their solution to each other and test how much of a balance has been achieved. Typical questions for the teams might be 'What happens if there is too much sun?', 'What happens if there are too many fish?' and so on.

Review The exercise can lead to a discussion on the balance in organizational systems.

Variation This could also be run as a large group exercise followed by a plenary discussion. Use a much larger sheet of paper for this exercise.

33   Questions, Questions!

Description   The exercise is for groups of three or more people. The participants must conduct a reasonably meaningful conversation but they can only ask questions. Each question must be answered with another question. Anyone answering with anything other than a question is eliminated.

Purpose   An amusing energizer that can test participants' patience as attempts to induce a response other than a question are parried.

Materials   None.

Duration   A maximum of 7 minutes – anything longer may test even the mildest mannered participant.

Procedure
1. Organize the participants into groups of three or more, three to five team members works best.
2. Explain that they are to hold a reasonably sensible conversation within the group but that they can only speak in questions. Each person speaks in turn and the conversation should rotate round the group.
3. Anyone who does not answer with a question, is adjudged by the other members to say something that bears no relation to the previous question or takes longer than five seconds to answer is eliminated.
4. The team 'winner' is the last person remaining.

Review   Discuss the pressure felt by individuals as the exercise continued.

Variations
1. The team winners compete at a plenary session final.
2. Instead of answering with a question the next person has to start their sentence using the last letter of the previous person's response. For example, a) 'Where shall we go today, Jane?' b) 'Elephants, let's go to the zoo and see the elephants.' c) 'Sure thing, it would be great also to see a bear.' And so on.

34   Quick Tower

Description   The teams plan and design a tower that can be constructed in 1 minute.

Purpose   The approach will explore problem solving, the defining of team roles and cooperation between team members.

Materials   Give each team the following identical materials.
Sheets of flip chart paper, A3 (or poster size) paper, and A4 (or letter size) paper.
Thin card.
Newspaper.
Paper clips.
A stapler and staples
Adhesive tape.
A tape measure for the competition phase.
A stop watch for the competition phase.

Duration   40 minutes.

Procedure
1. Distribute the materials and tell the teams they are required to design a 'free standing' tower that is capable of construction in one minute.
2. The teams have 30 minutes to design the tower and undertake dry runs.
3. After 30 minutes the teams assemble their materials for the build.
4. Simultaneously the teams build their towers for one minute.
5. The winning team is the one with the tallest tower.

Review   Examine the strategies that were adopted, how the team roles were defined and how team members performed during the 1 minute build.

Variations   None.

35   Scrambled Eggs

Description   Team members (six or more members per team) throw eggs to each other and try to catch them. This activity is best undertaken outside with participants wearing old clothes.

Purpose   This is a fun, energizing exercise with some risk.

Materials   A supply of eggs – preferably fresh.
String or something similar to mark out the course.

Duration   10 minutes.

Procedure
1. Use string to mark out two parallel lines about 4 metres apart.
2. Divide the group into two teams of six or more members. With more than 24 people, you may consider having three teams.
3. Half the members of each team to position themselves behind one marker line with the other half facing them behind the other line.
4. The members of both halves of each team stand in single file.
5. Select the team leader at the front of each row.
6. Give each team leader an egg.
7. At the start of the exercise the team leader must toss the egg to their waiting team mate opposite who has to catch the egg one handed. Two-handed catches are illegal and the team will be disqualified.
8. As soon as a player throws an egg, they step out of the way of the line so that their next team mate comes to the front of the line.
9. The game continues until every team member has had a turn.
10. When the team leader reaches the front of the line and successfully catches the egg the exercise is over. The first team to do so is the winner. Note: If an egg is broken or dropped the team must start again, using a new egg if necessary.

Review   Not necessary.

Variations
1. A potentially less hazardous exercise is to use hard-boiled eggs.
2. Russian Roulette Eggs. Provide a mixture of fresh or hard-boiled eggs and let the team leaders select an egg for their team. Note: The eggs could all be hard-boiled but the teams would not know that.
3. After one cycle of the exercise widen the lines by 1 metre and continue widening them after each cycle of the exercise.
4. Provide the teams with wire coat hangers, some cloth or netting,

bamboo canes, adhesive tape and other suitable materials to construct hand-held catching devices. Allow 15 minutes for construction and then use the widening line variant of the exercise to see which team can throw and catch over the greatest distance.

36   Stepping Stones

Description   Team members must cross the 'river' using cardboard stepping stones. Eight is the ideal team size.

Purpose   Energizing team exercise.

Materials   2 sheets of A4 card.
Masking tape.

Duration   10 minutes.

Procedure
1. Using the masking tape indicate the river's bank. The river should be at least 4 metres wide.
2. Ask half of each team to stand in a line one behind the other on one river bank and the remainder to stand facing them on the other river bank.
3. Give the first player of each team the sheets of A4 card. These are stepping stones and are used to cross the river.
4. Start the exercise. The first team member tosses one of the pieces of card a short distance away from them.
5. The player then steps onto the card and tosses the second piece of card in front of them and takes another step.
6. While balancing on the second piece of card the first piece of card is picked up and then tossed further across the river.
7. These steps are continued until he/she is across the river.
8. Using the same approach the second member of the team can then go back across the river.
9. This is repeated until all of the team members are on the opposite banks of the river to which they started.
10. If any team member loses balance and touches the floor with either a hand or foot he or she picks up the card and starts again.
11. The team which completes the task first is declared the winner.

Review   Not necessary.

Variation   All of the team starts on one side of the river and they all have to cross using three pieces of A3 card as stepping stones. Note: This exercise works for team sizes of six or eight members.

37   Tower Relay

Description   The teams, working in relay, are required to construct an exact replica of a tower.

Purpose   This is both a problem solving and team cooperation exercise while in competition with the other teams.

Materials   Lego® or similar construction blocks. Use 30 or more blocks per tower to make it sufficiently complex.
Tower bases (optional but does aid stability).
A table for each team's tower.
A container for each team's construction blocks.
A small table or chair for each container.
A clock or watch.
Paper for keeping score.

Duration   30–40 minutes, depending on team size and complexity of tower.

Procedure

1. In advance, construct a tower using a variety of sized and coloured blocks. Place it behind a screen or in a separate room.
2. Give each team the same blocks as the constructed tower so that participants can construct an exact replica.
3. Put each team's blocks in a container and place the container on a small table or chair located about halfway between the screened tower and each team's construction area.
4. Set up a table for each team on which the tower can be constructed. This is the construction area.
5. Ask team members to agree the strict order they will follow in visiting the concealed tower. The order should be written down so that it can be referred to at any time during the exercise.
6. On starting the exercise team members take it in turns to visit the concealed tower, collect a construction block at the halfway point and return to their construction area to build the replica.
7. The person who has collected the construction block is the only member of the team who can touch the team's tower during that 'go'. For example in a team of four (members A, B, C, D):

   ● Team member A visits the concealed tower and observes its construction.
   ● While A looks at the tower, B waits at the halfway point.
   ● As A returns and selects a construction block at the halfway point, B can go forward and look at the concealed tower. C

can then proceed from the construction area to the halfway point.

- A returns to the construction area and builds the replica while team member D observes.
- As team member B returns from the concealed tower C goes to the concealed tower, D goes to the halfway point and A becomes the observer as soon as B reaches the construction area.
- The process repeats itself until the tower is completed.

8. Once the team considers the tower is complete it is compared with the concealed tower. If it is not correct a sixty-second penalty is applied and the tower dismantled to the point where the error has occurred. The dismantled pieces are placed in the container at the halfway point and the relay process recommences until the tower is completed.

9. The winning team is the one who completes the replica in the least time, including penalties.

Review
The design of the exercise means that communication between team members is complicated by the relay and strategies will have to be developed to allow for information transfer and sharing. Focus on the processes that the teams set up to cope with this problem.

Variations
None.

38   What's the Value?

Description   Teams must guess the total value of the coins hidden in the palms of their opponents. Teams may be of any size but eight or less is best.

Purpose   Energizing team event.

Materials   A coin for each person.
A table that is long enough for the team to sit along one of its sides.

Duration   10 minutes.

Procedure
1. Sit two teams facing each other with the table between them.
2. Ask each team member to declare the value of the coin they will use for the exercise.
3. Decide which team goes first.
4. The members of the first team decide whether or not to put the coin in their right hand.
5. On the command 'Up' all the team clenches their right hand to make a fist and places it on the table.
6. The opposing team then decide the total value of the coins held.
7. The leader of the opposing team states the value of the coins and says 'Over'.
8. The teams, with the coins in their fists, turn their hands over and open their fists to reveal their coins.
9. The total value of the coins is calculated.
10. The exercise is then repeated for the second team.
11. The team whose guess was closer is the winner.

Review   Lead a discussion on the strategies used to guess the value and how people tried to bluff.

Variations
1. The teams can guess the number of coins to be revealed rather then the total value.
2. The teams can guess the number of coins and the total value.
3. Only one coin is used which is passed between team members under the table and the opposing team must guess who has the coin.

III

Large Group Exercises

Sometimes during an input session everybody's eyes start to glaze over or, worse still, somebody is quietly nodding off to sleep. I know there have been times when I have felt like dozing while attending a lecture. Everything seems to be a little surreal and you begin to feel detached from the proceedings. As a presenter the worst situation I ever found myself in was when I gave a paper entitled 'A View of the Desktop' to a team of oil industry IT managers. Presented in 1989 it examined my thoughts on the future of desktop computing environments and data management for the next decade. I had endeavoured, with the use of cartoons and humour, to make what could be a rather dull subject more digestible but I had forgotten about Murphy's Law. The law states – and I paraphrase – 'If anything can go wrong it will, and in a far more spectacular fashion than you could ever imagine.'

My session was immediately after lunch and as I sipped my mineral water I watched my audience have before-lunch drinks followed by wine with the meal and of course a little something to help the digestion. By the time we left for the auditorium they were all in an extremely contented frame of mind. It was going to be a challenge to engage them. But worse was to follow: as I entered the darkened lecture theatre a blast of hot air hit me. The air conditioning had failed and the room had become womb like, warm, moist, and dark. As I spoke I watched my audience struggle to keep awake with some just drifting off into a relaxed sleep.

When faced with these circumstances your only sensible course is to get the audience on their feet and undertake one or more of the exercises from the next session. Once the blood is moving again and the thoughts of sleep banished they will be considerably more receptive to the points you may wish to make. I rarely allow a task or presentation to go beyond forty to forty-five minutes without having a break for coffee or an exercise. Over the years I have found that a change of pace is often more stimulating than caffeine and now I prefer to use a combination of soft drinks, to reduce dehydration, and exercise to keep my audience lively.

39   Be It

Description   Participants walk round the room and the leader asks each person to become a specific object. Participants imagine they are the object and make an appropriate shape.

Purpose   This is a large group warm up exercise or energizing activity. It also can be used to develop individual creativity.

Materials   None, but this exercise is best done in a large room.

Duration   10 minutes.

Procedure   1. Ask the participants to stand and walk around. Depending on the number of participants and size of room you may wish to specify a direction.
2. Tell the participants that they have become a particular object, for example, a pair of scissors.
3. The participants stop moving and individually imagine they are the object and then make themselves into a shape that they feel shows the stated object.
4. Once the participants have formed their shapes ask some of them to state the type of scissors they represent, for example, kitchen scissors, surgical scissors, children's plastic scissors, and so on.
5. After a brief discussion about the objects they have created resume the exercise and suggest another object, for example, a table.
6. Continue the exercise for up to eight minutes.

Review   Discuss how participants felt when they were being an object.

Variations   None.

40   Connections

Description   A word association exercise, where participants are also required to have a good memory.

Purpose   Large group energizing activity with a twist because not all the rules are explained at the start of the exercise.

Materials   A pencil and paper.

Duration   5–10 minutes.

Procedure
1. Sit the participants in a circle.
2. Start the exercise by naming something. For example, 'Sausage'.
3. The participant on your left must then say what the word reminds them of. For example, 'Pig'.
4. Record each word but do not let the participants see what you have written.
5. The participant on their left then follows on with a connection for 'Pig'. For example, 'Farm'.
6. This carries on around the circle, with each participant adding his or her own connection.
7. Stop the activity once it has gone round the circle.
8. Then ask the first participant which was the last word.
9. The second participant then says which was the second to last word.
10. The exercise carries on round the circle with the participants working backwards.
11. If a participant gives a wrong word, provide the correct word.
12. Continue the exercise until it has gone right round the circle again.

Review   Discuss how participants associated words. Discuss participants' memory and whether it was fair to tell them the rules of the complete exercise at the half-way point.

Variations   None.

41   Imagine

Description   The participants imagine a cube, and the similarities, differences, and assumptions between the participants are explored.

Purpose   This exercise explores the use of language and assumptions.

Materials   None.

Duration   10 minutes.

Procedure   Start by asking the participants to sit in a circle or horseshoe shape.

1. Ask them to relax and shut their eyes. If necessary tell them that no tricks will be played on them.
2. Once they have settled and all their eyes are shut say to the participants 'Imagine a cube'. You may also wish to imagine a cube of your own.
3. Allow about 20 seconds and then say to them, 'Now, cut the cube in half'.
4. Allow another 20 seconds and then say to them 'Now, cut the cube in half again'.
5. Allow another 20 seconds and then say to them 'Now, get rid of the cube'.
6. Allow another 20 seconds and then say to them 'Open your eyes again'.
7. Allow about another 20 seconds and begin the review.

Review   Select a participant and ask him or her to describe the imaginary cube. You may need to prompt to find out if it was coloured, solid, rotating, and so on.

Select another participant and ask the same series of questions.

Continue this with a number of the participants.

Explore some of the similarities and differences in their cubes.

Continue the questioning by exploring how participants cut their cube in half. Down the middle? Diagonally? What happened to the halves? Did you use a tool? And so on.

Again explore the similarities and differences.

Repeat the same line of discussion for the second cut and again for how participants got rid of their cube.

If you had a cube in mind you may share what you visualized.

The review may continue with a discussion of language and the need for precision if thoughts and ideas are to be accurately shared.

Note: Occasionally when I have run this exercise a few participants have thought I said, 'Cue' or 'Queue' and were rather confused when they had to cut it in half! If this happens you have an additional opportunity to explore accent, distortion, and 'noise' when information is transmitted.

Variations   None.

42 Matchless

Description Participants remove matches from a pile of matches. The winner is the player who removes the last match.

Purpose This a large group energizing activity that involves some simple strategic thinking.

Materials Matches – 100 or more depending on group size. Craft shop matches are best.
A table.

Duration 5 minutes.

Procedure
1. Ask the group to sit in a circle.
2. Place the matches in a pile on the table.
3. State that each participant can take up to five matches from the pile and the object of the exercise is to be the person who takes the last match off the pile.
4. Select someone to start the exercise.
5. Continue until the last match is picked up.

Review Lead a discussion on strategies.

Variations
1. Vary the number of matches that can be taken from the pile with each go, that is, up to 5, up to 4, up to 3, up to 2, up to 5 and so on.
2. Generate the number randomly.

43   Mountain of Matches

Description   Group members take it in turns to build a mountain of matches on a wine bottle foundation.

Purpose   This is a group energizing activity.

Materials   About 120 matches. (Craft shop ones are best.) Each participant to have 6–10 matches.
An empty wine bottle or similar narrow necked bottle.

Duration   10 minutes.

Procedure
1. Form the group into a circle.
2. Place a wine bottle in the middle of the circle. You may stand the bottle on a table.
3. Place four matches across the mouth of the empty wine bottle.
4. The participants in the circle take it in turns to add one match at a time.
5. The aim is for the group to build the highest mountain possible.
6. If the tower collapses, the person who was attempting to put their match on the mountain places another four matches on the neck of the bottle and building then starts again with the next person in the circle.
7. If all the matches have not been used call 'Time' after 10 minutes.

Review   Discuss how people felt as they added their match, particularly as the mountain grew taller.

Variations   1.   To extend the exercise count the matches making the mountain and repeat the exercise during the event to see if more or fewer matches are used on subsequent attempts.

2.   The exercise can also be team based with each team trying to construct the highest mountain in an allotted time.

44   One-Minute Race

Description   Participants must walk between two markers in exactly one minute.

Purpose   This is a large group energizer where some interesting strategies may come in to play.

Materials   A watch. (Temporarily confiscate participants' own watches and hide all clocks.)
Masking tape for markers if the room is more than 12 metres long.
A tape measure or 3 metre piece of string for use as a measure.

Duration   2–3 minutes.

Procedure   1.   If the room is more than 12 metres long put down two strips of masking tape about 10 metres apart to be the start and finish lines.
2.   Ask all participants to stand at one end of the room or behind the masking tape line.
3.   When told to begin all the participants must move immediately and continuously towards the other end of the room or line. Anybody stopping will be disqualified.
4.   Their objective is to cross the finishing line (or the other end of the room) exactly one minute after the start.
5.   Any participant who stops moving or crosses the line too soon is eliminated.
6.   The nearest to the line after one minute is declared the winner.
7.   Start the race.
8.   After one minute ask all participants to stop.
9.   Measure if there is any doubt about who has won.

Review   Discuss strategies used to confuse other members and how the distance and timing were estimated.

Variation   Participants have to move at a constant speed for the whole minute.

45   Once Upon a Time

Description   Members of the group tell a story, but each person can only say one word at a time.

Purpose   The purpose is to develop group cooperation. It requires individual creativity, anticipation, and support.

Materials   None.

Duration   10 minutes.

Procedure   1.   Ask the participants to sit in a circle.
2.   The group is required to tell a story but each person can only say one word. The story is told clockwise round the group. The object is for the group to work together so that the story flows just as if one person alone were telling it.
3.   The leader starts the story with the words 'Once upon a time', then points to a person in the circle.
4.   That person adds one word. For example, 'A'.
5.   The person on their left then adds another word to the story. For example, 'Young'.
6.   The person on their left then says the next word. For example, 'Farmer'.
7.   The story continues to be built with words being added as it goes round the circle.
8.   Stop the exercise after a few minutes, 5 minutes at the most, or if the story comes to a natural break point.

Review   Discuss how individuals worked. Did they just say any word that might fit or did they have a view of the direction in which the story was moving?

Variations   1.   Split the group in half and ask the two sets of participants to stand in a line and face each other about 4 metres apart. Decide which set will start the story. The person at the end of the row says the first word, the person directly opposite says the next word and so on up and down the lines.
2.   A further extension is to stand the two lines with backs to each other.

46 Weather Walk

Description Group members walk round in a clockwise direction and act out walking through different weathers or environments.

Purpose This is a large group initial warm up exercise which can also be used as an energizer at any time during an event.

Materials None, but this exercise is best done in a large room.

Duration 5–10 minutes.

Procedure
1. Ask the group to stand in a large circle and face clockwise.
2. Instruct them to start walking in a clockwise direction.
3. After a few moments tell them that as they walk they will encounter a variety of weather conditions and to act accordingly.
4. After a few more moments tell the group that it is: raining, windy, foggy, very hot, very cold.
5. Then become more expansive in the descriptions. For example, 'It is a winter's day, a cold wind is blowing from the east, it is icy under foot, snow flakes are beginning to fall...'. Give the descriptions slowly and deliberately so that the participants have time to modify their mime as they walk.
6. Stop the exercise after 5–6 minutes.

Review Not necessary.

Variations The leader tells a story that incorporates initially the weather and then other activities like: opening a gate, boarding a bus, arguing with the conductor. It is generally a good idea to have prepared a story.

IV

Paired Exercises

You cannot have a smaller group than a pair of people and in both business and personal life we may often find ourselves, whether we like it or not, having to work in partnership. To me a good example of paired work is doubles tennis. Even though I do not play I always enjoy watching the doubles matches at Wimbledon, for when I see an excellent doubles team play they always visibly demonstrate all the skills necessary for high partnership performance. Watch a few sets and you will see being shown the complete gambit of skills including communication, perception, cooperation, problem solving, feedback, and support.

This section's ten exercises, although they do not include tennis, will touch on some of the aforementioned elements. Most are reasonably quiet exercises, though 'Back to Back Racing' can, as the name suggests, be extremely energetic with inter pair competition much in evidence.

47 A Couple of Things

Description   Each member of the pair discloses two facts that the partner does not know.

Purpose   This exercise concentrates on listening and feedback. It can be used as a warm up exercise prior to a team building activity or as an ice breaker. It should be kept non-threatening and relaxed.

Materials   None.

Duration   15 minutes.

Procedure
1. Ask each participant to think of two facts that they are prepared to disclose about themselves that the other members of the large group do not know.
2. Ask the group to pair up. Note: If the numbers are odd create a threesome with less time per person or, preferably, use yourself to make up the pair.
3. Each person has 5 minutes (3½ minutes for a team of three) to talk.
4. One person discloses their two pieces of information about themselves while the listener remains silent.
5. The listener then reports to the speaker what they have heard.
6. The speaker then feeds back on the accuracy of the listener's report.
7. The listener can then ask additional questions to discover more about the disclosed information.
8. After 5 minutes the roles are reversed.

Review   Lead a discussion on the power of active listening and the roles of feedback and disclosure in establishing relationships.

Variation   For teams of up to eight people a longer variant of the exercise can be employed as part of a team building exercise. Once the pairs have completed the listening and feedback session the team re-forms and each person feeds back into the group what their partner has disclosed. This feedback should last no longer than 1 minute per person.

48 Back-to-Back Racing

Description   Pairs stand back to back with their arms linked and race.

Purpose   A short sharp energizing session.

Materials   None.
If the room is too big, use masking tape or chairs to define start and finish lines.

Duration   5 minutes.

Procedure   1. Use either end of a large room or masking tape/chairs to mark the start/finish lines 6 metres apart.
2. Ask the group to form pairs and stand back to back behind the start line.
3. Ask the pairs to link their arms while remaining back to back.
4. On the command 'Go' the pairs race to the other line keeping their arms linked at all times.
5. On reaching the line the pairs come back without turning round. That is, each one of the pair has a turn at leading.
6. If a pair become untangled they must return to the start.
7. The first pair to cross the start/finish line is the winner.

Review   Not necessary.

Variation   This can easily be modified into a team exercise. The team stands in a line behind the line with the first and second members back to back. When the pair have completed the course the second member faces the front and links up with the third member in line. This process continues until all the team members have completed the course.

49   Backward Tower

Description Pairs sit back to back. One of the pair has a completed Lego® or similar plastic construction block tower that has to be described to their partner so that he or she can copy it exactly.

Purpose This exercise examines the use of language in problem solving.

Materials Plastic construction blocks. For each pair there should be a prepared tower using 20–25 pieces of various sizes and colours and exactly the same pieces for the member of the pair who is to construct the tower. Note: Use plastic bags to keep the tower components together. Freezer bags with openings that seal are excellent for this purpose.
A table and chair for each participant.

Duration 20 minutes.

Procedure
1. Build towers for half of the pairings. Bag the constructors' pieces.
2. Sit the pairs back to back with a table in front of each of them. Note: If you have a large group you can sit them in two long rows, but use a variety of tower designs.
3. Place the completed tower in front of one of the pair and give his/her partner, 'the constructor', a bag of plastic blocks to enable the tower to be replicated.
4. Tell the group that each pair have 10 minutes to replicate their partner's tower. Constructors have to ask their partners questions to determine how the tower should be built. Neither of the pair is allowed to look round to see what is on their partner's table.
5. Once the exercise starts the constructor asks his or her partner to describe the tower so they can construct an exact replica.
6. When they believe they have built an exact replica they compare towers.
7. If it is not exact the tower under construction is demolished and they attempt to build it again.
8. Stop the exercise once all the towers have been completed or after the 10 minutes.

Review Discuss questioning and answer techniques, particularly the use of open and closed questions.

Variations
1. Construct other easily recognized objects for replication. For example a boat, a car, or an aeroplane.
2. If there are a large number of pairs undertaking the exercise have them race. The pair with the first correct tower is the winner.

50 Double Talk

Description   Each pair decide on a paired identity, for example Salt and Pepper, Tom and Jerry, snakes and ladders and so on. The other pairs have twenty questions to guess the pair's identity.

Purpose   This is a creative energizer that explores questioning techniques.

Materials   None.

Duration   20 minutes.

Procedure
1. Form the group into pairs.
2. Each pair decides on an identity like salt and pepper or whisky and soda.
3. Select a pair at random to go first.
4. The remainder of the group asks questions in an attempt to determine the pair's identity.
5. The group has 20 questions to discover the identity of the pair.
6. Each question can only be answered with a 'Yes' or 'No'.
7. The questioning continues until someone correctly guesses the identity of the pair.
8. Either the pair who guessed correctly or another pair drawn at random takes the first couple's place.

Review   Discuss the questioning techniques employed and whether the group learnt as the exercise continued to structure their questions so that they more rapidly identify the pair.

Variations   None.

51   Flight of Fantasy

Description   The pairs build an aeroplane which must 'fly' along a piece of twine.

Purpose   This is a creative problem solving exercise for the pairs, which can become energetic as the pairs compete to produce the fastest aeroplane.

Materials   Sufficient chairs and 6 metre lengths of twine or parcel string for each pair. Alternatively, provide two chairs and two lengths of twine/string to enable a knockout competition to be run.

Also provide each pair with:

A plastic or paper cup.
2 drinking straws.
5 sheets of A4 paper.
Adhesive tape.
Scissors.

Note: You can always supply additional materials for the exercise. Sometimes the extra resources complicate the problem which in itself can become an interesting discussion point.

Duration   10–15 minutes depending on the number of pairs and whether a knock out competition will be run.

Procedure
1. Form the group into pairs.
2. Give each pair a set of construction materials.
3. Ask each pair to construct an aeroplane that will 'fly' by being blown along the twine. One end of the twine is to be tied to the chair, while the other is held horizontal and taut by one member of each pair.
4. The pairs have 7 minutes to construct their aeroplanes.
5. The aeroplane is threaded onto the twine or string.
6. The aeroplanes are lined up at the start and on the word, 'Take off' the member of the pair who is not holding the twine or string blows the aeroplane along it.
7. The first aeroplane to reach the other end is the winner.

Notes:
1. Watch out for twine or string not held horizontally.
2. Creative teams may design something to improve the blower's performance, for example, a cone. That is acceptable and indicates 'outside of the box' thinking.

Review   Discuss the designs, particularly if a cone or similar was employed to enhance blower performance.

Variations   None.

52   Matchbox Collection

Description   Pairs are given a matchbox and must fit into it as many different objects as they can.

Purpose   This is both a creative and energizing activity.

Materials   A matchbox for each pair. Note: They should all be the same size or those with the smaller ones will complain!

Duration   20 minutes.

Procedure   1. Form the group into pairs.
2. Give each pair a matchbox.
3. Instruct the pairs that they have to fit as many different articles as they can find into the matchbox. Stress the word different, 50 matches are not allowed.

4. Define where they can scavenge.
5. Start the exercise and stop it 15 minutes later.
6. Late arrivals will be disqualified.
7. The winning pair is the one with the most articles in the matchbox.

Review   Discuss how the pairs went about the exercise and how creative they were in finding items.

Variation The pairs must find the most unusual item they can fit in a matchbox. They should give reasons for their object's uniqueness.

53 Perceptions

Description Pairs examine the same picture and compare their perceptions.

Purpose The aim is to simulate participants' contact with a situation and examine their personal perceptions and filters.

Materials A photograph for each pair of participants. Note: The photograph should show people undertaking some activity. Ideally the picture should include people of different genders, ages and/or races.
A pencil and paper for each participant.

Duration 25 minutes.

Procedure
1. Ask each pair to look in silence at their picture for one minute.
2. After a minute each should think about what they liked and disliked in the picture, how they felt about what was going on, and what the people involved in the picture were feeling.
3. Ask them also to see the picture in terms of what they think is happening now and to imagine what happened before the photograph was taken and what happened after the photograph was taken.
4. The pair should then spend 10 minutes separately recording their impressions.
5. After 10 minutes the pair should discuss their responses. They should examine the similarities and differences and share what they think are the reasons behind their responses.

Review Explore and discuss first impressions, our personal filters, and how we organize what we see.

Variations None.

54 Personality Swap

Description Pairs swap personalities and then explore what led them to focus on particular traits. The exercise should be conducted towards the end of a three-day plus event or among people who already work together.

Purpose This exercise provides an opportunity to feed back and explore behaviours in pairs or small teams.

Materials None.

Duration 20 minutes.

Procedure
1. Ask the group to form pairs from people who have worked together for a few days during the event or worked together for some time prior to the event.
2. Explain that the pairs are responsible for each other and that honesty and truth form the basis of the feedback being given.
3. The first member of the pair behaves for 3 minutes as if they were their partner.
4. After the session the second member feeds back what they observed and asks follow up questions to explore the behaviours they have seen.
5. The first person expands on any points that were raised.
6. The pair then swap roles.

Review Discuss the giving and receiving of feedback and how individuals felt.

Variation If the pairs are part of a small group the pairs may feed back to the small group the behaviours observed and how they felt while undertaking the exercise. The group can also formulate some rules for the giving and receiving of feedback.

55 Synchro Clap

Description Pairs develop a method of recognition and communication by synchronized clapping.

Purpose This is a warm up exercise for pairs who will be working together or it can just be used as an energizer. It can also provide an opportunity to explore the effect of noise on the communication process.

Materials A pencil and paper.

Duration 5–10 minutes.

Procedure
1. Organize the group into pairs.
2. Allow the pairs 3–4 minutes to develop a clapping pattern by which they can recognize each other. Note: A short, easy to remember repetitive pattern is best.
3. Separate the pairings and stand them 6 metres apart with their backs to each other.
4. Rearrange one line so that the pairings do not know their relative positions.
5. Stand facing one of the lines and point to an individual.
6. The person being pointed at starts to clap using their agreed pattern.

7. When a person in the other line recognizes the pattern they start to clap with the intention of synchronizing with their partner.
8. Make a note of which pairings were correct and when more than one person tried to synchronize.

Review   Discuss how the pairs determined their code, how easily they recognized each other and the need for careful listening.

Variations
1. Have more than one pair clapping at a time.
2. Blindfold one of each pair with the objective that they must home in on their partner's clapping.
3. Blindfold both with the objective that they must find each other.

Note: All of these variants lead to a discussion about the impact of noise on the communication process

56   Table Tennis Roll

Description   Pairs work cooperatively to roll a table tennis ball between them on two pieces of string.

Purpose   This exercise enables pairs to work in cooperation to achieve a simple goal. The exercise can be used as a warm up to more demanding paired work.

Materials   For each pairing:
A table tennis ball and two lengths of string each about 1.5 metres long.

Duration   5 –10 minutes.

Procedure
1. Ask each pair to hold a length of string in each hand between them.
2. Tell them to hold the string taut between them, like a pair of train lines, with the strings close enough together to enable the table tennis ball to roll along them.
3. Place the table tennis ball on the string near the hands of one of the pair. (A third person may help here.)
4. On the word 'Go' one of the pair lowers their hands slightly so that the ball can roll to the other person.
5. As it reaches the other person's hands the pair change stances so that the ball will now roll in the opposite direction and back to the start point.

6. The pairs attempt to achieve as many complete rolls between each other within a set time, for example 3 minutes.

Review   Explore how the pairs worked together to maximize the back and forward rolls.

Variation   To increase the energy level the exercise can be run as a race. For example, the first pair to complete ten lengths is the winner. If a ball falls off the train lines the pair starts counting from the beginning again.

V

Individual and Creative Thinking Exercises

How we go about solving problems has always been of particular interest to me. Some people take a predominately logical approach whereas others appear, as if by magic, to pluck their intuitive solutions from thin air. To me a mixture of hard logic combined with a liberal dose of intuition and a penchant for ignoring the rules will almost always deliver the best possible solution. I always think of the way Francis Crick and James Dewey Watson sought to unravel the DNA helix: the former was methodical and structured whereas the latter was coming at the problem from all directions. Working individually they may never have achieved a resolution but their combined approaches solved the problem.

The exercises in this section do not pretend to pose such a mind-stretching question but a number of them will provide an opportunity to explore hard and soft approaches to problem solving as well as exploring problem definition and 'thinking outside of the box'. All of them will introduce a slower pace into the proceedings and are quiet – unless, that is, participants start fighting over the glue pot as they build their collage!

57   Collage

Description   Participants build their own collage to describe a problem or desired state.

Purpose   This approach allows individuals to express their feelings visually about an issue or situation.

Materials   A large supply of newspapers and magazines.
A pair of scissors for each participant.
Glue and/or adhesive tape.
A sheet of flip chart paper for each participant.
Coloured pens and markers.
A table or working space for each participant.

Duration   50 minutes.

Procedure
1. Provide each participant with a sheet of flip chart paper, scissors, glue, and an identified working area.
2. Ask the participants to create a picture illustrating either a problem or issue or the desired state following the resolution of a problem.
3. Set out the magazines and newspapers in a central location in the room and let the individuals select their own cuttings to make a collage.
4. Allow 30 minutes for the participants to complete their collage.
5. Participants take it in turn to describe their collage.

Review   Explore how individuals undertook the task and how straightforward they found the activity. Discuss any problems that people had when undertaking the task.

Variations   None.

58   Find the Letters

Description   The participants must complete the series of letters.

Purpose   This is a brainteaser that can lead to a discussion about hard and soft thinking, problem formulation and how people process data. It can be used in conjunction with **That's Logical** (Exercise 65).

Materials   A pencil and paper for each participant.

Duration   5 minutes.

Procedure   1.   Prepare the table shown below on a work sheet, flip chart or OHP acetate.

O	T	T
F	F	S
S	?	?

2.   Show the table to the participants and give them the following instruction: 'Reading from left to right complete the series by inserting the missing letters'.

3.   Answer: One -Two-Three-Four-Five-Six-Seven-Eight-Nine.

Review   The solution requires soft thinking rather than logical thinking. Discuss how the data were tabulated and whether or not that contributed to finding the solution. Did the participants hear the phrase about reading from left to right?

Variations   None.

59   Find the Number

Description   The participants determine the rule that identifies the colour for each shape on the abstract drawing.

Purpose   This is a logical problem solving exercise and can be used as either an energizer or in an examination of the ways that we think about problems.

Materials   A copy of the picture for each participant.

Duration   10 minutes.

Procedure   1.   Prepare a drawing similar to the one below.

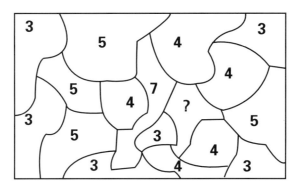

2.   Distribute copies of the drawing to the participants.
3.   Ask the participants to determine value of the shape indicated with a '?'.
4.   Answer: 7. It is the number of the adjoining shapes which determines the value of the shape.

Review   Explore how the rule was determined.

Variation   Replace numbers with colours. It needs a little more thought in the construction of the picture but adds an interesting dimension, as participants will have to double decode to arrive at the answer.

60   Five-O-One

Description   Not darts, but instead the participants must do some arithmetic to arrive at a score of 501.

Purpose   This is a cerebral exercise that is useful to slow the pace down after a particularly energetic session.

Materials   A pencil and paper for each participant.
Note: If you are not very good at arithmetic, have a calculator available to check the answers.

Duration   15 minutes.

Procedure
1. Ask the participants to write down eleven numbers from 0 to 9 inclusive with no number featuring more than three times in their list.
2. Once they have all written down the eleven numbers ask them to combine them to form a new set of numbers, none of which should exceed three digits. For example, the first list may be 3, 7, 7, 4, 2, 1, 8, 6, 3, 9 ,5 which in turn could form a new set of 3, 72, 471, 39, 8, 65.
3. Ask the participants to use all the numbers to reach 501 by addition, subtraction, multiplication, or division. Note: The use of brackets is allowed but dividing by zero is not.
4. Allow a maximum of 10 minutes to complete the exercise. The winner is the nearest to 501. For example, from the numbers above you could make 471+39 (= 510) −8 (= 502) − (72–65)/3 = (500.33).

Review   The various methods employed to reach the 'answer' will be examined during the exercise. What strategies, if any, did participants adopt to determine their approach?

Variation   Only allow calculations that result in whole numbers. For example 9/3 (= 3) is acceptable, 10/3 (= 3.333) is not acceptable.

61   Four in a Row

Description   A lateral thinking problem where participants arrange four coins or counters in a row.

Purpose   This exercise can be used as an energizer and to explore 'thinking outside of the box'.

Materials   Six coins or counters for each participant.

Duration   5 minutes.

Procedure   1.   Set out the six coins or counters as shown in the diagram.

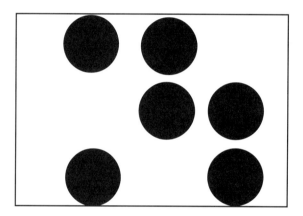

2.   Give the participants six counters each, or let them use their own coins, and ask them to set out the coins as described above. Note: A prepared sheet for each participant indicating the counters' starting positions ensures that everybody starts from the correct initial state.
3.   Give the following instruction 'Move two counters (coins) to make two rows of four counters'.

4.   Answer:

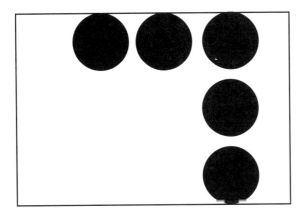

There are two counters on top of each other at the corner.

Review   Discuss problem definition and boundaries. Assuming a participant solved the problem, how did they make the mental leap?

Variations   None.

62   Grid Locked

Description   Participants are required to draw a line which crosses each segment of the grid but does not cross itself.

Purpose   This is a lateral thinking exercise that may be used as an energizer or to lead a discussion into problem solving.

Materials   A pencil and A4 paper for each participant.

Duration   5 minutes.

Procedure   1.   Draw the grid shown below on a flip chart, worksheet or OHP and ask the participants to draw a similar grid on their paper.

2.   Instruct the participants that they are to draw a line that crosses each line segment of the grid but without crossing itself.
3.   Answer:

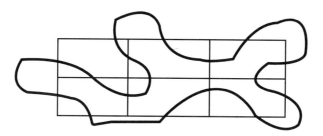

Review   Discuss how the participants approached the problem and explore how 'thinking outside of the box' may help in problem solution. They are required to go outside the box several times.

Variations   None.

63   Memory Drawn

Description   The participants have a number of simple sketches to remember and draw.

Purpose   A memory exercise that can be used as an energizer or as a starting point for an examination of how people remember things.

Materials   Six simple drawings.
A pencil and A4 paper for each participant.

Duration   10 minutes.

Procedure   1.   Prepare six simple drawings on a flip chart or separate pieces of A4 paper or card. For example, three of the drawings could look like this:

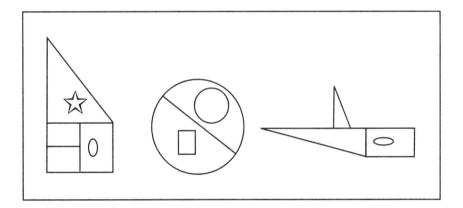

2.   Number the drawings.
3.   Let the participants study them for 90 seconds and then remove or cover up the drawings.
4.   The participants must draw each picture as accurately as possible from memory.
5.   Stop the exercise after five minutes, let the participants reveal their sketches and compare them to the originals.

Review   Discuss the strategies the participants used to memorize the pictures.

Variations   1.   Colour the pictures to add a further degree of complexity.
2.   Run the exercise as a paired session with one of the pair looking at

the pictures on the flip chart, which is out of their partner's sight, and then describing them for their partner to draw. This is a mixture of memory and communication.

64 Multipliers

Description This is a brainteaser where participants have to work out how many ways the word Multipliers can be spelt.

Purpose This is an energizing activity that requires a combination of visual perception and mental agility.

Materials Pencil and paper for each participant.

Duration   5 minutes.

Procedure   1. Prepare the triangle drawn below as a work sheet, acetate for OHP, or on a flip chart.

```
        M
       UU
      LLL
     TTTT
    IIIII
   PPPPPP
  LLLLLLL
 IIIIIIII
EEEEEEEEE
RRRRRRRRRR
SSSSSSSSSSS
```

        2. Show the triangle and ask the following question 'Starting with the letter M at the top of the triangle, reading downwards, and always using an adjacent letter, how many different ways can you form the word MULTIPLIERS?

        3. Answer: Ten steps are needed to get from the M to the S in MULTI-PLIERS. Each time there are two ways you can follow. So there are 2^{10} = 1024 ways that you can form the word MULTIPLIERS.

Review   Not necessary.

Variation   You may use any appropriate eleven-letter word, for example your company's name, the event name, and so on. Take care with the spacing between letters to ensure that it looks like a triangle so that the two alternatives are visually obvious.

65   That's Logical

Description   The participants must find the missing number using logic. That is, find the rule that applies to the table.

Purpose   This is a logical, but not necessarily straightforward, exercise that can be used to contrast hard and soft thinking. It can be used with the **Find the Letters** (Exercise 58) to help illustrate the different kinds of thinking.

Materials   A pencil and paper for each participant.

Duration   5 minutes.

Procedure   Prepare the table as shown below on a work sheet, flip chart, or OHP acetate.

1	1	1	1
1	3	5	7
1	5	13	25
1	7	25	?

Display the table and give the participants the following instruction: 'Complete the table by logically finding the missing number'.

Answer: The number is determined by adding the numbers above, to the left, and diagonally to the left. Thus the missing number is 13+25+25=63.

Review   Discuss finding the rule or pattern when problem solving. Also explore the risks of looking for patterns, if the pattern should change.

Variations   None.

66   Tricky Tray

Description   A trick exercise where participants are led to believe that they have to remember the items on a tray whereas in reality they have to observe the person who is carrying the tray.

Purpose   This approach is an energizing activity with a strong observational slant and also examines active listening.

Materials   A tray with about twenty everyday objects on it.
A pencil and paper for each participant.
A watch.
An assistant to carry the tray. Note: If possible the assistant should be someone the participants have not seen before. However, even if someone they know is used it is common for participants to mistake much of the detail. For example, they may describe the clothes the assistant was wearing the day prior to the session or what they normally wear.

Duration   5 minutes.

Procedure
1. Place the 20 items on a tray in another room.
2. Tell the participants that they are about to undertake an observation exercise.
3. Ask your assistant to come into the room holding the tray.
4. The assistant stands in front of the group.
5. Tell the group, 'You have 60 seconds to memorize what is in front of you'.
6. After 60 seconds ask the assistant to leave.
7. Once the assistant has left the room tell the participants they have to try to remember as many things as they can about the assistant. For example, colour of hair, clothing, jewellery, and so on.
8. The participants make their list.

Review   Discuss how the task was explained to them and explore their assumptions.

Variation   Ask the participants to list what was on the tray as well as what the assistant looked like.

VI

Closing

As an event draws to a close it will offer an opportunity for reflection, feedback, and planning for the future. The longer the event the more likely it is that those first impressions now have something more substantial to support or dismiss them. Teams may have developed to a point where they are producing excellent work and most participants will have formed some views on their fellow members.

These exercises provide an opportunity for participants to feed back to each other and to the event leaders. In addition to the exercises providing feedback 'Autobiographies' and 'Goals for the Future' also enable individuals to do some first pass planning so they can move forward from the event. I always value what is said during the feedback session or stuck on the wall as a result of 'Message in a Bottle' as it always provides a rich context to the scorings that are given on the obligatory company feedback forms.

67 Analogies

Description Working in small groups participants provide analogies about themselves and each other and then discuss them.

Purpose A creative and amusing exercise that provides some insights into the personality and behaviour of participants during the event.

Materials A prepared list of analogies for each group.
A pencil and paper for each participant.

Duration 30–40 minutes depending on group size.

Procedure
1. Prepare the list of about 10 wide ranging analogies. For example

   If X were a dog, what sort of dog would he or she be?
   If X were a means of transport, what sort of means of transport would he or she be?
   If X were a flower, what sort of flower would he or she be?
   If X were a colour, what sort of colour would he or she be?
   If X were a vegetable, what sort of vegetable would he or she be?
   And so on.

2. Distribute the list to each group of participants.
3. Ask the group to spend 5–10 minutes preparing a list of analogies for each member of the group, including themselves.
4. Ask the group to select one person at a time and then share and discuss the analogies. The reasoning behind the analogy may be explored during these discussions.

Review A plenary discussion examining the process, how people felt and whether individuals viewed themselves in a similar light to their group members.

Variations None.

68 Appreciative List

Description Every member of a large group (12 or more members) writes a sentence of appreciation to each other.

Purpose A way for a large group to say words of appreciation to each other.

Materials A pencil and A4 sheet of paper, preferably lined, for each participant.

Duration 15 minutes.

Procedure
1. Ask the participants to sit in a circle.
2. Ask them to write their name at the top of the sheet of A4 paper.
3. Ask each of them to think of something positive that has happened to them during the event.
4. Ask the participants to write the positive statement at the *bottom* of the sheet of paper and fold it over so it cannot be seen.
5. Ask the participants to pass the sheet clockwise to the next person.
6. Ask that person to write down at the bottom of the sheet a positive statement about the person whose name is at the top of the sheet.
7. Ask them to fold over the sheet and pass it clockwise to the next person.
8. This continues until the sheet returns to its owner.
9. Ask the sheet owners to write a positive statement about themselves at the top of the sheet and then unfold it and examine all the statements.
10. Allow a few minutes for silent reflection.

Review Not required.

Variation Participants may add their names to the statement.

69   Autobiographies

Description   Working in pairs participants think of a title for their autobiography, which is then discussed by the pair.

Purpose   An opportunity for participants to look to the future, share it with each other, and obtain their partner's views.

Materials   None.

Duration   15 minutes.

Procedure   1.   Organize the group into pairs.
                 2.   Tell them they are responsible for managing their own time.
                 3.   Ask the participants to think of a title for their autobiographies.
                 4.   In pairs they describe their title, explain what it means and discuss it.
                 5.   They then help each other determine the three key targets they must achieve during the next three years if the autobiography is to be realized.

Review   None.

Variation   Extend the exercise to include what sort of picture they would have on the front cover. After the title has been discussed each participant should try to visualize what the cover picture would be like. Each then discloses their own thoughts about the picture and explores the similarities and differences. Allow an extra 10 minutes.

70   Fortunately, Unfortunately

Description   A small group closing off exercise where the participants say why it has been fortunate for them to have been together for the event.

Purpose   It provides a structure and is an alternative to the group just saying their quick farewells.

Materials   None.

Duration   5 minutes.

Procedure
1. The group sit in a circle and the first participant makes a true statement about the event beginning with the word 'Fortunately...'.
2. The person on their left then says something true about the event but this time they begin with the word 'Unfortunately...'. Note: A double negative may be used to make the statement positive.
3. The exercise continues until the group runs out of statements to make about the event.

Review   Not necessary.

Variation   One person in the group captures the comments on a flip chart under the two headings and the small group feeds their thoughts back at a plenary session.

71 Goals for the Future

Description   The participants work in pairs to help each other formulate their future goals.

Purpose   This approach helps anchor the event and assists participants to identify their future direction.

Materials   A pencil and paper for each participant.
Each pair will require a watch or clock to time the sessions.

Duration   40 minutes.

Procedure

1. Ask the participants to organize themselves into pairs. Note: If there is an odd number have one group of three and allow an extra 15 minutes for the exercise.
2. Tell them that each member of the pair will take it in turns to be the 'client' and 'consultant'.
3. The consultant's task is to help the client concentrate on three to five future goals. The goals should be a mixture of career and personal ones that are in balance.
4. The consultant starts by asking the client to spend up to 5 minutes describing what they would like to be doing in five years' time.
5. The consultant then spends up to five minutes asking questions to more fully understand exactly what the client wishes to achieve.
6. After the questioning phase the consultant says the following to test their understanding 'In five years' time you wish to A - ..., B- ..., C-...' and so on, to a maximum of five statements that encapsulate what the client wishes to achieve.
7. The consultant and client agree on the statements.
8. The consultant then asks the client to explain to them in 4 minutes or less what they must do in the next year to achieve their five-year goal.
9. The consultant asks questions for up to a further 4 minutes to understand what the client wishes to achieve and again makes a series of up to five statements that encapsulates the client's goals for the next year.
10. The consultant and client agree on the statements and a date when they will review progress.
11. The roles are then reversed.

Review   The plans may be reviewed within any existing small work groups.

Variations   None.

72 Message in a Bottle

Description Participants write messages concerning the event and place them in a bottle, which is then opened up for the messages to be displayed on a notice board.

Purpose This is an alternative way of collecting end of event feedback. It can be anonymous but the output can still be displayed.

Materials A large, 2 litre plastic bottle.
Pens and A5 sized paper/card for each participant.
Blu tak® or similar plastic adhesive.
A sharp knife for opening up the bottle.
A large display board.

Duration   15 minutes.

Procedure   1. Tell the participants that they are on a desert island and that the only way they can send information about the event to others is by using a bottle.
2. Display the bottle and place it in the centre of the group.
3. Give each participant paper or card and pens.
4. Ask them to capture their thoughts and ideas about the event and the other participants and place them in the communal message bottle. If the message is to a particular individual the sender should put their name on it. General messages and comments may be made anonymously.
5. Pass the bottle round the group so they can put their messages in it.
6. When there are no more messages to be put in the bottle cut it open and display the messages on the board (or wall if a board is not available).
7. Allow participants time to look at the board.

Review   Not necessary.

Variations   None.

73 My Friend

Description The participants say their farewells to each other using song titles.

Purpose An amusing and creative way of closing off an event. It is best used for events of two days or longer and with a group of ten people or less.

Materials None.

Duration 5 minutes.

Procedure
1. Ask the participants to form a circle.
2. Select someone to start or start the exercise yourself.
3. The closure starts off with the chosen first participant saying to the person on their left 'You are my friend because' followed by a song title, for example 'You make me feel like dancing'. As the song title is said he or she shakes the other person's hand.
4. The person on the left whose hand has been shaken then proceeds counter clockwise round the circle and shakes the hands of all the other participants.
5. As the person shakes their hand they also give a song title, for example, 'It's a long and winding road', followed by the next person, and so on, until they have progressed round the circle.
6. When they return to their starting place they shake the hand of the person on their left and the cycle starts again until everybody has done a circuit.

Review Not necessary.

Variations None.

74   Personal Column

Description   The participants compose a short advertisement about the event for inclusion in the personal column of a newspaper or magazine.

Purpose   This can be the first phase of the closing off section of an event. It combines creativity and fun with some quiet reflection about the key points of the event.

Materials   A selection of newspaper articles. Note: Broadsheets should be between one and two columns in length and tabloids between two and three columns in length.
A pencil and paper for each participant.

Duration   20 minutes.

Procedure
1. Fold the newspaper articles so that the topic is not obvious to the participants.
2. Give pencil and paper to each participant.
3. Let the participants select their article.
4. Tell the participants that they have 15 minutes to produce an advertisement of no more than 20 words for the event. Apart from two 'free' words of their own choice they must only use words from their cutting. The words can be used in any order from the article and must be circled as they are used.
5. After 15 minutes ask each participant to tell the group the source and nature of the article from which they have produced their advertisement and to read out their advertisement.

Review   Not necessary.

Variation   Use it as a small group exercise.

75   Positive Strokes

Description   Pairs explore giving and receiving positive feedback based on the event.

Purpose   This approach helps affirm positive behaviour of individuals during the event. In addition it provides practice in how to be more positive in dealing with people after the event.

Materials   A pencil and paper for each participant.

Duration   15 minutes.

Procedure
1. Ask the participants to form pairs.
2. Each member of the pair thinks of and writes down examples of the positive behaviour they have observed from their partner during the event. Allow 3–5 minutes for this phase.
3. Each participant reads out examples of the positive behaviour. As they read them out their partner tries out responding with affirmative behaviour. For example: nodding and smiling, maintaining eye contact or saying things like 'Thanks for telling me', 'Great', and so on.
4. The participants then check how they felt about giving and receiving positive responses, what helped them and what did not.
5. The pairs then discuss the approaches they will employ away from the event to both give and receive positive strokes.

Review   A plenary session can be run to examine general approaches to giving and receiving positive strokes.

Variations   None.

Managing the Training Process

Putting the Principles into Practice

Second Edition

Mike Wills

What they said about the first edition ...

'It is about time that professional trainers had a book that contains all they need to know, written in a clear concise and thought-provoking way. This is it.'
IT Training

'I wish it had been available at the time I became a trainer.'
Leslie Rae, The Training Officer

A comprehensive practical guide to managing all aspects of training, from programme creation to implementation and monitoring success rates. It offers flexible strategies for adapting training to meet the demands on today's professionals. The book takes into account all the complexities of modern business practices and how trainers and training managers should plan and then implement an overall training process in their organization.

This new edition retains popular features of its predecessor, for example, the flow chart structure, and some of the original themes which have now been developed further. It also covers some of the latest developments in the ever-changing world of training and development, including quality assurance of training suppliers; training self-audits; using managers and others to deliver training; the line manager's role in the training process; the relationship of the training process to the learning organization; the use of competencies in the process; training networks; and the Internet and training.

Gower

Planning and Designing Training Programmes

Leslie Rae

The quality of the planning will be instrumental to the ultimate success of any training or development programme, yet as the demands on today's trainers are constantly changing, the pressure to devise effective training, often at short notice, is increasing.

This book by one of the UK's leading training authors looks in detail at the entire planning process, set very much within today's challenging corporate context. Following the book will enable any trainer to devise a professional training and development programme, by:

- identifying and analysing training needs
- designing and planning a programme to meet them
- designing and planning the individual sessions within it
- evaluating success - at the start, during, and at the end of the programme.

Included are all the considerations a trainer needs to be aware of, ranging from skills assessment and learning styles, to relative benefits of on the job and off the job training, and the value of different types of training formats. Finding time for proper evaluation is crucial too, and Leslie Rae highlights a wide range of options. Also included is a unique index of available training resources.

This exceptionally practical structured approach will help any trainer to shorten the planning time involved whilst improving the quality of that preparation.

Gower

Team Development Games for Trainers

Roderick R Stuart

If you're involved in designing or delivering interpersonal skills training you will know that there are two perennial problems. The first is finding material that matches your objectives. The second is finding material that will be unfamiliar to the participants.

The 59 games in Roderick Stuart's collection have not appeared in print before. Based on the author's experience with a wide range of organizations and participants, they cover the entire gamut of skills associated with team development, including assertiveness, communication, creativity, decision making, influencing, listening, planning, problem solving and time management.

Each game is presented in a standard format, with an indication of objectives, timing and group size, detailed step-by-step guidance for the trainer or team leader, and ready-to-copy masters for all participants' material. An index of objectives makes it easy to select the most suitable items for your training needs and to compile complete workshops or more extensive programmes. In addition the author provides a four-stage model that relates learning to the requirements of the workplace, and a set of checklists for facilitating the learning process.

Gower